Acknowledgments:

"when you've tried": *Weber Studies*, Special Poetry Supplement, 1999

"do this:": *Red Crow Review*, Spring/Summer 1999

"there are some perfectly": *Graveworm*, featured poet section, http://www.graveworm.com, June/July 1999

"some night": *Graveworm*, featured poet section, http://www.graveworm.com, June/July 1999

"what do you do": *Graveworm*, featured poet section, http://www.graveworm.com, June/July 1999

"there are some people": *Graveworm*, featured poet section, http://www.graveworm.com, June/July 1999

"sometimes you suspect": *Graveworm*, featured poet section, http://www.graveworm.com, June/July 1999

"fluorescent": *Entre Nous*, September 1999; *Phoenix Press*, Runner, March 1999

"imagine what": *Midwest Quarterly, Great Plains Poets Issue,* Summer 1999; *Phoenix Press*, Runner, March 1999

"you spend": *Entre Nous*, March 1999

"approaching": *Blind Man's Rainbow*, Vol. IV, III Feb/March 1999; *Phoenix Press*, Runner, March 1999; *Weber Studies*, Special Poetry Supplement, 1999

"the earth": *Phoenix Press*, Runner, March 1999

"when unexpected": *Phoenix Press*, Runner, March 1999; *Weber Studies*, Special Poetry Supplement, 1999

Dirt

Michelle Paulsen

Hope and Allen Publishing
P.O. Box 926
Grants Pass, OR 97528

Published by Hope and Allen Publishing
P.O. Box 926
Grants Pass, OR 97528

Printed in the United States of America
ISBN 0-934264-10-4

"…instinctively they stuck to the Small Things. The Big Things ever lurked inside. They knew that there was nowhere for them to go. They had nothing. No future. So they stuck to the small things."

-Arundhati Roy

Dirt

For Erik and Sparky

The nature of things

the sugar
maple may be
sweet, but she's not
innocent skin
bright as a
lamp without
shade, she arrives
late, eating and drinking and
sinning and speaking
of an indian
summer. an aging
starlet, painted
face to the
crowd, she can't keep her
insides from
oozing out

in morrisons
novel, a small
black girl
prays
for her dolls
blue eyes;
only
a child
would face
trading the
pitch of
sleep
for the dreamy
tidal pull
of the sea

imagine what
its like to
sleep through a
rainstorm, and
wake in
the morning,
trapped.
imagine this
occurs on a
regular basis, but
is in no way
predictable. how
do you
know when you've
plugged enough
tires, alone
on a
gravel road,
wondering if the
jack will collapse?

disillusioning,
the high
desert, an ancient
sanctuary, almost
devout, the light
thin and clear lifts
weight from
shoulders. there is a
reason for the
birthplace of
belief. but wanting
to believe, landing
there, third wish
consumed, the light
wavers, and the
sand, coveted for
cleansing covers all
tracks and chokes the day

there are two
kinds of
mountains,
frequent and
insistent, the
common hill
steals the
landscape. charming,
the surface
teeming with
life, the
jealous adolescent
confines the
horizon. it is a
close compartment, a
myopic existence at
too low
an elevation.
but there are places
where there are peaks
only in the distance,
majestic barren mountains
that might be
mirage, but exaggerate the
expansiveness of the
terrain. insurmountable,
they instead inspire
the illusion
of soul

you gladly
give your last
weekend, simply
to see the fall
colors. grounded,
acres of majestic
lollipops, brilliant
rage against
the inevitable
barrenness to
come. from a different
perspective, indistinguishable
from the family
room carpet your
parents insisted
the height
of fashion
in the
fifties

its no
accident; the most
dangerous thing
to look at,
is when
the moon
crosses the
sun, and even
the smallest
child has to
swallow hard,
and stare
at the
ground, to
not go
blind

Location, location, location

there are
some perfectly
human
constructs; for
instance, consider
las vegas,
if everyone were
dead

the discrimination is
northward, winter is a
grave occasion-
only what is
six feet under
survives. for six
months it is master
of all it
surveys. At once
assassin and
antibiotic its
cleansing conquest is
complete. southward
there are no such
certainties. the cold
sterilization never
comes, all things
rankle and
fester and
abhor the
white
of day

maybe its
because it is in the
middle of
everything, somehow
protected on all
sides. or maybe
its because the
land is
flat; there is a
place where you can
achieve balance.
there is no necessary
inflection in
voices, as everyone
picks up their
children and heads
home

fluorescent
light has done
this to
me, i want long
hair, a short
skirt. i want to
rush next
door and throw
my arms on his
shoulders, hip-sway
and music. i
want to throw my
head back, and
laugh

the earth is
different here, a
devil's food
layer cake,
blood-red
scarlet and crimson.
valleys of
saints drawing
imaginary lines; a
stratified shelter
against an army
of sinners, a
laminated oasis
in the
Sun

even now, missouri
is a border
state, its kingdom
come, sam
clemens, joined the
confederacy and then
deserted, for
personal reasons. the black
suit from
chicago is too
dark, the skirt too
short and suggests
life too
frankly. and white fights
the oppressive
hear, but only
tourists can
carry it
off

approaching
thirty, in a
plane over the
pacific, no
children with
the child
of an
obese opera
singer who,
since boyhood,
has had
visions
of the
wrong end of
girdles. california
behind us, the flight
plan suggests
we do not
stop until west
becomes east.
with nothing
on the
horizon but
water, I am
beginning to be
suspicious of the
meanings of
words

ever been
somewhere
with more
sheep than
people? to be
honest, its hard
to tell the
difference

when you've tried
to live
here long
enough, you begin
to understand the stubborn
shiftlessness of the
place. the
clay doesn't allow for
absorption, and
nothing can take
root. the effort
stains hands blood
red, which only wears
but never
washes off

there's a certain
insanity caused
by being
landlocked,
as if the
brain can't get enough
oxygen. or perhaps
its the other missing
element- the one
which allows us
to fly

sometimes
it takes
a perfect
place
to see
a perfect
truth; in
a hotel
room in
nassau, for instance,
looking out
at the melting
crayon sea, when
all you can
hear are the
cries of the
'spring break' crowd,
and the
moans of
your partner's
porn
behind you

Inner terrain

do this:

stand in
a deep
pool, hold your
breath, and
do as many
somersaults as
you can. then
do one more.
when you
emerge, brave
the primary
incoherent
gasp

you spend
a lot of
time in
museums, pacing
the sterile
rooms, looking
for life. in the
art institute
there is a large
black canvas. how
to learn
to see
like this,
an appropriate
color for
everything

there are some
people you meet
who simply know
too much,
and if they're
young, they are
impossible
to look
at, without
giving in

when you
sit, alone
with your
pen, do you
wonder at
James, or
any other
novelist:
how to
spool out
consciousness
into a
delicate
web? instead,
words only
come when
there is nothing
else left, akin,
you believe,
to the
sensation
of vomiting
drano

sometimes
you suspect
you were
born or
branded
with a luminous
scarlet letter;
there are those
few who,
with ultra-violet
eyes, even
in an
unfamiliar crowd,
recognize you
and read
right
through

didn't anyone
ever tell you
not to listen
to music through
headphones or drink
alone?

some night
when you
are finding
it hard
to remember
your name
let alone
behave
as if it
doesn't matter,
walk away
from the
oblivion we
naively call
sleep

why do those
we consider good
with the
camera, in the
search for real
toads, so often
dismiss the
rainbow, blink and
breathe in
black and
white?

and so
the animal
claws its
way out,
and what
was
transparent
now runs
blood
red

what do
you do
with the
sorrow, when it
burns through
like an
iron?
cut off all
oxygen?
bury it with
dirt? its
a shallow
grave, and
some have the
eyes of
thieves

it starts
with a sickness
at the back
of your
throat; and
when you
reach, it's the
numbness you
crave, not the
antiseptic

the secret
is this:
the moment
(we all crave)
when everything
falls
into place, is
the end
(ah! too late!)
of this jigsaw
life

there is a
certain naïve
euphoria in the
audience at a
concert; while
those responding
to the sound
and the fury
would never
make that
mistake

funny
how we give
anything to
have someone
stare
at our
guts all
over the
page

there are
those of
us who
walk about
seething;
the mere
scratch of a
fingernail or
sharp look
makes us
publicly bleed
out

try to
demonstrate that
half instant
when you
wake in entire
dark, and
don't know
where you are

practicing as a
child, each piece
had to be
perfect. a slight
hesitation, a
slip, you had to
start over. something
reassuring about
repetition, the resolve
to be
redundant, old enough
now for the
music to
move you, you
yearn for that
satisfaction. but
reiteration has become
reverberation, stir and
shudder. and
there is no
renewal in
reproduction

technology is
a suspect
teacher; we
learn that
blood identifies
the one,
though we
all need
to make
eye contact
to believe

there is a
look that
heals the
exhausted spirit.
it is the most
common thing
in the world

Critters, and other parasites

when unexpected
guests show up for
dinner, each
woman, alone
in her
kitchen, knows
how to stretch the
meal

·

at a
distance, he appears
innocent, his freckled
face, religious
awkwardness, easy
answers. But
the consequence
of being
alone, close
enough to
feel is contradictory,
a gravity induced
vertigo, a
Goliath magnet
in his
chest

her eyes
are nearly
swollen shut.
'what is
wrong? has someone
hit you?
i don't see
any marks. they
must be
very good
at what they
do.' its not like
vomiting, the
relief of
dry heaves. she
fights all
day to
stop, her throat
nearly as
swollen from
all the
swallowing.
'what is wrong
with you?'

pregnant
you wake
early one
mourning in
blood, and tell
no one.
that afternoon,
a child
comes and insists
you change
your pink
lipstick (of ten years);
she gives you
a new
color. and
later, when she is
raped, you conceive
there is no
new color
to give
her

my grandmother
bought the first
microwave, and one
summer morning
taught me
how to
cook. bacon; i
remember cooking
all she had-
two whole packages.
my mother hated
to cook, you see, and
felt it necessary
to also deny
me the
displeasure of the
act. funny thing;
i love to
cook, and i'm a
vegetarian

your neighbor's
daughter is
19, and you're
not. saturday,
on your
knees, scrubbing
stains and
receiving carpet
burns, she asks why
you don't have
a baby. its
september, but still
ninety degrees, and the
air is too
thick to
answer

sometimes after
class they
ask 'can you help
me with my word
choice?', 'do you
understand me?',
are you
my angel?

ah , i
will never be
the same. raised in
religion, i bought
the tapes, was even asked
out by the doctor
of psychology. but the closest,
best, nearest is the sign
'all aboard,
at the
disneyland
railroad,
main st.
frontierland,
tomorrowland station'

kiss my
ass- how to
remember someone
who said
that in my
defense, as well as
hers – who would
just as soon
ride up a dirt
road with a
bucket of
margaritas, laughing at
rain so
thick we couldn't
see, and
shaking, want to
light up
anyway. older
than my mother, a
nurse besides –
no sense that
there's nothing
to do

and allen ginsberg's
dead, only a few
weeks before i finally give
my fist
reading. lonely
old courage-teacher,
the wine's not
helping, america is
a series of
infomercials, and i crave
the pure
the burning
neon of a
supermarket in california, the
simple singular
light

in a
dream
last night
my mother
was someone
else, a bitter
redhead who
hated my long
blond hair, she
cut and
burned me, until
she proved
i was
crazy, for
not being
a copy
of her

the day comes
when you need
to understand
your name,
and the
answer, 'we
weren't prepared
for a
girl,' you can
never share
with your baby
brother,
michael

for years,
she writes
poetry her
mother refuses
to read; what
will others
say? the thing
is, the handwriting
is the
same, and the words
stream down
the page with no
shoulder to
catch them

your baby
brother writes,
he says
'its always
darkest just before
it goes completely
black'; you
haven't seen
him in
ten years, but
you know
he's no longer
blond

About the Author

Dirt is Michelle Paulsen's second book of poetry. Her first book, *What Wells Up*, was published in 1997 by the Edwin Mellen Poetry Press. She also has work in dozens of journals, and on the Internet in hypertext form. She teaches at The University of Missouri-Rolla and Concordia University- St. Louis Center, and can be reached at paulsens@yahoo.com.

Additional copies of this book may be ordered from the publisher:

Hope and Allen Publishing
P.O. Box 926
Grant's Pass, OR 97528

http://www.hopeandallen.com
info@hopeandallen.com